BIG AL'S
OFFICIAL GUIDE TO
CHICAGO·ESE

"Loving Chicago is like loving a woman with a broken nose."
—Nelson Algren

BIG AL'S OFFICIAL GUIDE TO CHICAGO·ESE

by Bill Reilly

Contemporary Books, Inc.
Chicago

Illustrations by Bill Stebbins

ACKNOWLEDGMENTS

This book would have been a lot tougher to write without the help of all Chicagoans who talk this funny way. Especially, the author wishes to thank Velva Lee Heraty, Sgt. Hubie Heraty, CPD; Dave Osborne, Osborne & Tuttle; Don Klimovitch, *Chicago* magazine; Lee Flaherty, Flair House; Mad Mimi Wilson; Eddie "Dutch" Vogel, my Godfather; George Filipetti; Mike Royko, of course; and Helen, who hung in there.

Front cover illustration by William Shallop

Published by Contemporary Books, Inc.
180 North Michigan Avenue, Chicago, Illinois 60601
Manufactured in the United States of America
International Standard Book Number: 0-8092-5608-8

Published simultaneously in Canada by
Beaverbooks, Ltd.
150 Lesmill Road
Don Mills, Ontario M3B 2T5
Canada

What Didja Say?*

"So I go to my *Chinaman* and tell him I want to get this *Stanley listed*, see? But then I find out he's *heavier* at *22nd & Wentworth* than I am, like straight from the *fif' floor*. He's even *double-dippin'*. Next thing you know, he puts the *jacket* on me. I get *vised out* and he winds up wit' all the *cream*, and I'm back at *Monkey Ward* wit' me *dukey*. So that's why I'm puttin' the *arm* on you, *Willie*, for that *big one* you owe me and, maybe, some upstairs *clout* from your *goo-goos*."

*NOW, DON'T BE LEFT OUT OF IT. Be able to understand what the guy on the next barstool is talking about. The words in italics are the clues. Look 'em up!

Foreword by Mike Royko

It was a good ten years ago that I first met Reilly. I was sitting in a bar, minding my own business, when I heard someone complaining about something controversial he had read in the paper that day. Since I had written what he had read, the criticism was obviously directed at me.

As his complaints grew louder, I did what I often do in such cases. I took a coin from my pocket and slid it down the bar to him.

He said: "What's this?" I said: "It's a refund for the price of the newspaper. Now let me be."

The guy jumped up. So did his two pals. All three cocked their fists, twisted their faces into menacing expressions, and began making threats about the kind of mayhem they were going to perform on me.

I looked them over. Individually, they didn't appear to be top contenders. Well-dressed, with blow-dried hair, like most of the overpaid stewbums who came into the place, which was a hangout for advertising and newspaper types. There wasn't a scar or lump on their faces.

But three to one are not good odds, even if I threw bottles and ashtrays and swung a chair.

The bartender responded to the crisis by loping to the far end of the bar and busily washing glasses that were already clean. They don't make bartenders like they used to.

The three hostiles started to move forward, and I picked up my beer bottle, while mentally vowing that in the future I would always sit near an exit.

Just then I heard a hard, flat voice say: "OK, you sons of bitches, let's go."

I looked to my left and this total stranger was standing there. He was on the balls of his feet, bouncing slightly. His shoulders were slouched and shoved forward to protect his chin, which was tucked in. Both arms were bent in the way that makes it easier to throw left and right hooks.

"Who are you?" I asked.

"I'm Reilly," he said.

"Pleased to meet you," I said.

"We can talk later," he said.

One of the three jerks said: "There's three of us, buddy."

"I know," Reilly said, "which means you assholes are outnumbered."

They stared at his face. It wasn't the kind of face you wanted to cause to frown. I've seen faces like that before—back when Chicago still had gymnasiums where boxers trained.

The three jerks weren't sure what to do. So Reilly helped them decide.

"Before we get started," he said, while doing a fancy bit of footwork and throwing a couple of practice hooks that whistled, "I think I ought to tell you something. I used to do this for a living. And I was good at it. So if you want to make it real interesting, we can make some side bets. Like which one of you hits the floor first."

One by one, their hands dropped to their sides. And they slowly turned to the bar, downed their drinks, picked up their change, and got up to leave.

"Hold on," Reilly said.

"Huh?" one of them answered.

"Let's have the money back. You don't deserve a refund. It was a good column."

So I began my friendship with Bill Reilly, ex-pug, writer, adventurer, world traveler, and not a bad traveling companion if you have to walk down to the O.K. Corral.

And did I mention "Chicagoan?" That above all. Oh, how this man loves the city—the sights, the sounds, the people, the legends, the folk tales, the crooks, the hustlers, the elbows in the ribs, and the hands in the pockets. If you ever took Reilly out of Chicago and dumped him in the countryside, he'd probably die of clean air poisoning.

For years, he's talked about writing a book that contained some of the flavor of Chicago. Not for the money, although any writer who doesn't make that at least a small consideration shouldn't be allowed near his typewriter. But more to return to the city some of the fun that the city has given to him.

He's finally done it, and I think he succeeds in making it fun.

Reilly has an ear for the way Chicagoans talk. As in any big city, the natives have their own language. Some of it is street talk; some political talk; some soul talk; some an Americanization of the old country talk that parents brought with them.

It isn't exactly poetic, although it can be, as when Nelson Algren used it. And it's not subtle, as with the English writers of English.

It's crude, earthy and, in some cases, pretty foul. For example, my all-time favorite Chicago sentence was once uttered by the desk sergeant in a South Side police station, when a prisoner was banging his head on the cell door because he didn't like the quality of his accommodations. The sergeant said: "Fuck the fucking fucker."

And, to outsiders, it can sound like a secret code, as when a payroller in City Hall says: "There was a beef from a goo-goo because I took a little fresh, and I was gonna get vised, but my clout squared it." Which, of course, means: "A reformer complained that I was taking bribes, and I was about to be fired, but my political sponsor hushed it up."

Reilly has done a book on the way his Chicagoans talk. (We would not suggest that people talk this way on Astor St., of course.)

It might not be the definitive work. And I'm not sure that the schools will put it on their required reading lists.

But, like Reilly, it's fun, it's tough, and it has punch. If you study it, you can go in almost any neighborhood bar in Chicago and be understood.

And should you have any problems while you're in these bars, look around for a curly haired, stocky Irishman who looks like he takes facials with a washboard. If it's Reilly, you'll probably survive.

By the way, the three stiffs returned that money. And Reilly said:

"I saved you the trump, so you buy the beer."

INTRODUCTION

One of the really frustrating problems faced by strangers to Chicago—although never mentioned in the tour guides—is the language barrier. Non-Chicagoans are often stumped when they try to communicate with the natives in their own tongue—Chicago-ese—a peculiar, inbred jargon full of words and expressions found nowhere else. Here, for the first time, is a handy dictionary that will help to overcome that problem; it will enable anybody not only to understand the local dialect but, with a little practice, even to speak it themselves—be an *insider*.

Also included, for the first time, are the location and the local vernacular for the city's geography and topography; many of its landmarks and institutions, as well as its neighborhoods, ethnic villages and minitowns; and their often rough and bawdy history as only Chicagoans know it. You'll find the little area maps, especially, an invaluable aid for getting around.

For crime buffs and the curious—and who isn't where the Windy City is concerned?—there's a special bonus: **Bugsy's Illustrated Chicago Crime Tour.** This section takes you directly to these storied old spots and tells you what happened, accompanied by on-the-spot photos taken when history was being made. Now, you can walk the once "holy ground" yourself. You can take your own pictures, see how these places look today, compare 'em to the old photos.

Chicago-ese, in short, gives you a treasury of outrageous facts and lore about the most American of America's cities. Its people and its politicians, its crooks and its cops. The fascinating bits and pieces that gave it, and still give it, its unique flavor. Where it all is and how it got there. Consider it your Chicago Survival Handbook.

Special note: You may find talking Chicago-ese a bit awkward at first. Before you plunge into it, it's a good idea to listen to the natives. See how they handle it, and especially study their mannerisms as they talk, because that has a lot to do with it. Note that true Chicago-ese is delivered mostly out of the side of the mouth, sort of confidentially, as if the speakers don't want to be overheard. Often this is accompanied by a kind of *knowing*, almost conspiratorial nod of the head. Policemen, bartenders, and aldermen are good role models. Here are a few more tips:

Phonetically, the tone is flat and nasal, almost harsh. The *th* sound, such as in "this," isn't too important. You sort of glide over it. You use an *is*—close to, but not quite like the low-brow *dis*. "Esses" aren't a big deal, either. Mute them. And the word "mayor," for example, is pronounced "mare," like the horse's wife. Trail off your "R's."

Spend a few minutes in front of a mirror. Start by putting your hand up to the side of your mouth and saying, "Ch-cah-guh." That's the correct pronunciation of the city's name. Next, go to a complete sentence. Try, "Who's 'ah big McGaffer in 'is ward?" Work for speed. Slur words. Chicagoans talk fast. But stay with it. In no time at all, you'll be talking like a 1st Ward Precinct Captain.

Word of warning: Don't stay here too long! You might find yourself falling in love with the naughty old girl. Although Big Al's old town traditionally gets a bum rap from the rest of the country—as a rough, dirty, Mafia-ridden kind of place—it's also a big, warm, livable town with some of the most kind, generous folks this side of your Mom and Dad. However, as a stranger in town, remember to keep your eye on the meter, cut the cards, and always ask for 20% off the top.

Guide to Chicago-ese: The Dictionary

Alderman
A big belly. A beer belly, such as traditionally found on Chicago aldermen.

Alley Apple
(Black) A brick—like for throwing.

Alley Sweeper
Machine gun.

Alligator Clips
Burglary tools, especially used to bypass burglar alarms.

Area One
Chicago's biggest and toughest police/crime area. Headquarters at 51st and Wentworth, south side. Includes the 1st, 2nd, 3rd, and 21st police districts, running north to the Chicago River.

Arm
To "put the arm on" someone, in Chicago, is to ask them for a favor. Usually it is asked of a friend or associate and is of a fairly "heavy" nature. Often it is a favor you have coming. It can also work in reverse; i.e., "Stanley never worries about the two o'clock closing time in his joint. He's got the ward committeeman on his arm."

Back O' The Yards
General area around and behind the old Union Stockyards, once a famous Chicago landmark. Original Irish/Polish/Lugan "packinghouse" Chicago. The big yards are now largely defunct; the giant packers—Swift, Armour, Cudahy, etc.—moved out with the changing times. Storied power base for many of the city's machine-Democrat politicians. Now largely a Latino and loosely heterogeneous racial mix. Halsted Street from around 2200 north to 4200 south is the main stem. Try Schaller's Pump, 3700 block on Halsted—they've still got a good steak. (*See* Bridgeport, Canaryville, 11th Ward.)

Bad Breath
Gary, Indiana.

Bad Ride
(Black) A good ride. Snazzy car; good wheels.

Bagman
The guy who picks up the illegal payoff. Collection man; drop man for graft, juice, vigorish, payola. (*See* Gaffer.)

Barrelhouse
Gin mill. Shot and beer joint. Cut-rate liquor store with a bar, "muskie" and a juke box. (*See* Skid Row, Uptown.)

Big John
John Hancock building, at Michigan and Delaware, near north side. World's second tallest.

Big McGaffer
(*Irish/Polit.*) Local clout man. The big honcho on the job or in the ward. The man to see for a favor, job, handout, ticket-fix, garbage pickup, or reduction in your water taxes. (*See* Clout.)

Big One

(Hood/Polit.) A thousand clams—a grand. Like in, "Well, gimme a coupla big ones and mebbe we can talk." Also, sometimes a big score or favor you have coming.

Big Stan

Standard Oil building. On Randolph Street, just east of Michigan Avenue, a few blocks south of the river.

Billy Goat

Popular newspapermen's hangout under Michigan Avenue at Hubbard. Ask for a "doobla-chiz"—that's a double cheeseburger. (The late John Belushi, of "Saturday Night Live" fame, is said to have based part of his "Greek Restaurant" sketch here.)

Black Hand

(Ital.) "La Mano Nera." Extortion. An honored tradition employed for generations by terrorist bands of the *Mafia* and the *Camorra* in Italy and Sicily. Imported to Chicago in the 1890s and used to prey on well-heeled immigrants in the Italian quarter. The procedure was time-honored and simple. A penciled note with the crude drawing of a black hand, a dagger, or a skull and crossbones was slipped under the victim's door, along with a demand for money. The victim generally paid promptly. If he didn't, he got a bomb or a *stiletto* some dark night. During a 30-year period in Chicago, some 400 murders were attributed to the Black Hand, by police and by various organizations set up to combat the gangs. One of these organizations was the White Hand, made up of law-abiding Italian citizens in the quarter. Many a big-time Italian gangster of the '20s served his apprenticeship in the early Black Hand gangs. (*See* Deadman's Tree, Little Italy.)

Bloochie

(Polish) Any awkward, unwieldy object. Something without handles, making it difficult to pick up or steal, like a piano. An object that would challenge the Panczko brothers, Chicago's oldest and most celebrated thieves.

Bloody Maxwell

Once called "the wickedest police district in the world." Old slum and crime area bounded by Harrison Street on the north, 16th Street on the south, Wood Street on the west, and the Chicago River on the east. An incredible stewpot that took in much of The Valley, The Patch, Little Italy, and the Maxwell Street ghetto. Its population of more than 200,000 included large and usually warring factions of Russians, Greeks, Lithuanians, Poles, Irish, Italians, and Jews. It had more saloons, bagnios, gambling joints, and just plain dives than not only Chicago, but America has ever known.

Bloody 19th

The old 19th ward on the city's near west side, just southwest of the loop. Once the heart of Chicago's steaming Little Italy; before that, an immigrant Irishtown. So named because of its turbulent election history, violent even by Chicago standards. Setting of the bomb-throwing "aldermanic wars," fought between the camps of John "Johnny De Pow" Powers, the resident alderman, and Tony Di Andrea, a political maverick attempting to break the Irish stranglehold on the ward. Powers, an Irish saloonkeeper, political fixer, and crook, was said to be the only man in the city council who would steal a hot stove—no small compliment from his brother aldermen in those days. Di Andrea, an ex-counterfeiter, bank robber, and defrocked priest, was backed by the six "Terrible Genna Brothers," no Sunday school kids themselves. By the time the smoke cleared, in 1921, more than 30 bodies had been left strewn about the ward, including Di Andrea's. (*See* Deadman's Tree, Little Italy.)

Blue and White
Squad car.

Boodle
(Polit.) Graft. Gravy. All the illegals and quasi-legals that come with the office of a Chicago alderman, by tradition and divine right. This ranges from patronage to free parking and free food and from "early bird" financial deals to lucrative voting rights on sewer, transportation, education, and real estate transactions.

Bowl of the Hawk
Bowl of chili.

Brick
(Hood) Ten cartons of cigarettes, usually without a tax stamp and at a pretty good price. Don't ask where they came from.

Bridgeport
Old Irish settlement around 35th and Halsted streets, on the southwest side. Called Bridgeport because it was the terminus of the Illinois-Central canal, dug by Irish immigrant labor in the 19th century. Center of the city's 11th ward, fiefdom of much political clout and patronage for the last 75 years. Chicago's last four mayors—except Lady Jane, who had close ethnic/political ties—were Bridgeport boys. It's not all that Irish anymore—mucho Latino. (*See* Back o' the Yards, Canaryville.)

Bubbly Creek
A once noxious branch of the Chicago River near the old Union Stockyards. Once used by the packers as a sewer for their offal. So fetid it got its name from the gases that bubbled to the surface, creating a miasma that practically asphyxiated the citizens. The only creek in the country that you could walk across on top of the water.

Bucktown
Babushka city—old Polish town. Grab a Milwaukee Avenue bus around 400 north and ride it all the way, past Division, Armitage, Fullerton, all the way out to where the cemeteries begin. See the real Chicago. Actually, it's not all that Polsky anymore; becoming heavily Latino, Black, a classic big city melting pot mix. Unfortunately, you'll find most of Chicago's rich and colorful ethnic neighborhoods only a memory. But you can still eat a good *pierogi* at Jake's Restaurant and Lounge, in the 4800 block on Fullerton. (*See* Bucktown map.)

Bughouse Square
AKA "Mini-Fagville." Officially Washington Square, but no real Chicagoan ever calls it that. A small, wooded park on the near north side, just off the Rush Street nightlife district, it's bounded by Clark, Dearborn, Walnut, and Chestnut streets. Once, and hence the name, an open-air/free-speech forum for the bushy-haired. Marxism, Fascism,

For a Taste of the Real Chicago, Visit the "Minitowns"

Here are three of 'em—rich, yeasty slices of the city. The "old" neighborhoods that put you in touch with the town's real character better than any guidebook ever could. Neighborhoods that are changing themselves, along with the city, even as you read this—changing culturally and ethnically from day to day, block to block. Meet Chicago!

Old Town.
Wells Street is the main drag. Pick it up at Division, 1200 north, just west of LaSalle. Follow Wells to Armitage, 2000 north. The hub is at North Avenue, 1600 north. Note lots of side-street spillover, especially along Clark and Armitage. Don't wander too far west; it can get a mite hairy. (*See* definition of Old Town.)

New Town.
The big streets in this "village" are Clark and Broadway. Take Clark Street north, straight out of the Loop, to Fullerton, at 2400. Follow Clark up to Diversey, 2800, and you're about in the center of things. (Clark and Diversey is also Gay Corner, if you're so inclined.) On that corner you'll see Broadway sort of dogleg off to the right. Follow it to around Belmont, 3200, where the action peters out. (*See* definition of New Town.)

Bucktown.
This trip is easy. Just stay on Milwaukee Avenue all the way—that's Bucktown's Broadway. This hallowed Chicago street starts at Lake Street, just northwest of the Loop, and cuts a colorful swath across the northwest part of the city, all the way out to the slurbs (see definition). Like we keep telling you, though, most of Chicago's great old ethnic neighborhoods are fast disintegrating, Bucktown along with them. But, if you move fast, you can still see a little slice of this one. Take Milwaukee Avenue to Fullerton, 2400 north, and walk Logan Square. That was the western edge of the original old Bucktown. (*See* definition of Bucktown.)

Old Town

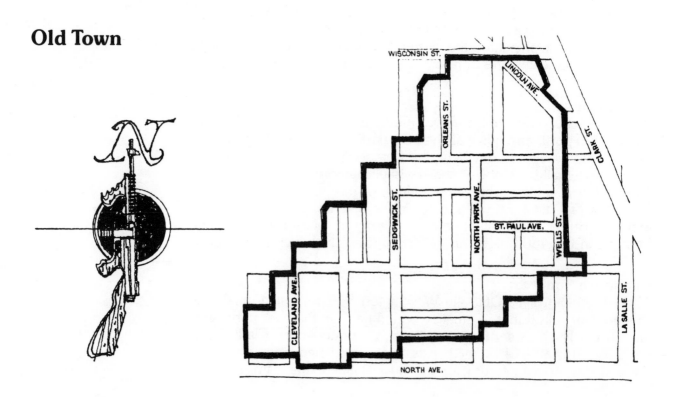

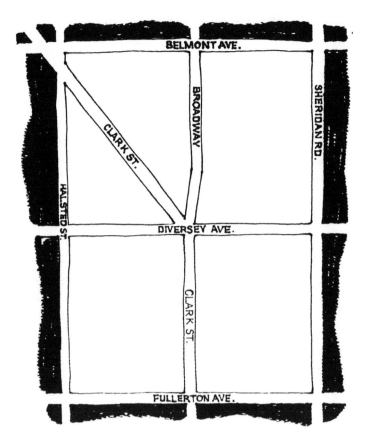

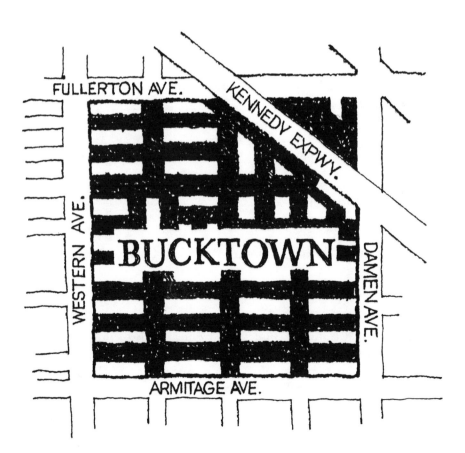

free love, snake oil—they were all pitched from the soap box here on any warm summer night. Today mostly a pickup-assignation spot and cruising area for the town's less affluent gays. John Gacy, Chicago's latest mass murderer, added considerably to his score here.

Bull Fever
(Hood) Having a sixth sense where the heat is concerned, especially as to *their proximity*. A form of ESP, developed over the years by many old cons, whose services are valued highly by the syndicate. Unfortunately, most Chicago cops can always spot hoods with bull fever . . . they keep looking over their shoulder.

Bungalow
A peculiarly Chicago building style, originally borrowed from the Prairie School of architecture. Hundreds of thousands of these small, squatty, single-family brick and frame dwellings were thrown up by builders in the teens, twenties, and thirties. To see them, drive out into the "neighborhoods," southwest, west, and northwest of the downtown area. See solid, blue-collar, tax-paying Chicago.

Button Man
A soldier. A "made" member of an organized crime family or syndicate.

Cabrini Green
City's most notorious federally funded housing project. A gang-infested, low-rent, vertical slum, despite the efforts of the many honest but beleaguered tenants to make it halfway livable. Lady Jane and her hubby made a show of taking an apartment and living there for a brief period, protected by half the city's police force. Their stay lowered the crime rate temporarily. Jay did hang in there and is doing a good job setting up athletic programs. Starts at Division and Clybourne, near northwest side. Don't go there.

Cage
(Black) High school.

Camping Out
Living anywhere outside Chicago.

Can You Stand a Stop?
Are you clean? Can you *afford* a pinch? What are you carrying? What about your record?

Canaryville
Small piece of the "ould sod," squeezed into a sliver of turf on the southwest side. Find it between Halsted Street and the Pennsy tracks, Root and 49th streets. For some reason, this confine stayed solid turkey (see definition). But, for bejasus sake, don't confuse it with Bridgeport, its Irish rival next door. Mike Royko, the *Sun-Times* columnist, once

did and almost got himself publicly shillelaghed. (*See* Bridgeport, 11th Ward, Royko.)

Cannon
The pickpocket who moves in to do the actual *picking,* after the "bumpers" and "movers" have set up the mark.

Capable Kid
(Hood) Hit man.

Captain's Man
Collection man for the police captain in the district. He picks up the "drop." (*See* Bagman.)

Catch the Bus
Go home. You struck out.

Cemetery Vote
Time-honored Chicago political practice of voting the ward's recent corpses, culled from the obituaries. (Dead people still on the voter registration lists.) It's helped swing many a close election. (*See* Stinger.)

Ch-cah-guh
Correct pronunciation of the city's name.

Chicago Typewriter
(Trad.) Thompson submachine gun, aka *chopper.* The original tommy gun, three models of which came out of World War I. The Chicago Typewriter was the smallest and handiest. Introduced into gangland warfare in the '20s by Frankie McErlane, a psychopathic killer who worked for the southwest side Oberta-Saltis mob. McErlane used it to rub out "Spike" O'Donnell, a competitor. (*See* Dingbat.)

Chinaman
(Polit.) Political sponsor. Your personal clout, your man upstairs. Like in "Sonny, if you want to make lieutenant in the Fire Department, don't be a hero; get yourself a Chinaman." (In New York it's a Rabbi.)

Chinatown
City's biggest Chinese district. Follow Clark Street as it turns into Wentworth, south out of the loop. The hub is at 22nd Street. Once the outskirts of Chicago's old Levee (redlight district). But don't go there looking for a *real* Chicago Chinaman. Go to Bridgeport.

Chop Shop
"Midnight garage" where stolen cars are taken and cannibalized for their parts. Parts are then sold, through prearranged outlets, at a fat profit—often on specific part demand. A good chop shop can make

your car disappear in two hours. Chicago is the birthplace of the chop shop—car butcher to the world. Park here with care.

Chum
(Hood) Political ally. Pal-o-mine.

City Motto
Urbs in Horto. Translation: "Where's Mine?"

Clean
(Black) Sharply dressed. Cool.

Clock
(Hood) Used in sentences like "Put a clock on him." To study an intended hit victim's daily habits and schedule in order to pick out the best time and place to knock him off.

Clout
(Now Generic) Political pull. A Chicago contribution aimed at enriching the mother tongue. (*See* Heavy, Fif' Floor.)

Come Up
(Hood) Raise the cash or else. Like in, "Come up with it, Clyde, or we take one of your eyes."

CPT
(Black) Straight time. You're clean.

Cream
Usually graft. Goodies—over the counter or under it.

Cry Baby
(Cops) Kid con artist who uses the "I lost my carfare and can't get home" pitch to scam nice old ladies. Cries buckets of tears on demand. Don't listen to the little bastard.

Dan Ryan
Car accident—fender bender. Chicago's Dan Ryan expressway, which skirts the Loop going south, is the nation's busiest and perennial leader in accident stats.

Dead Man's Corner
The corner of Sangamon Street and 14th Place in the old Bloody Maxwell Street police district. More police and criminals were killed there than at any other site in Chicago (not to be confused with Death Corner; *See* definition).

Deadman's Tree
An ancient poplar on Loomis Street, in what was once the heart of Little Italy. Black Handers (see definition), in the old days, posted the names of their intended extortion victims on its trunk. These little billets-doux, embellished with the traditional skull and crossbones, or daggers, were usually sufficient by themselves to collect the cash, without resort to mayhem. For crime buffs, this tree was still standing at last reports, though sickly. (*See* Little Italy and maps.)

Death Corner
The intersection of Oak Street, 1000 north, and the old Milton Street, now Cleveland, on the near north side. Notorious dumping ground for gangland and Black Hand bodies, in the early teens and twenties, as the area was changing into a "new" Little Italy. Favorite slaughtering ground of a professional assassin known as the "shotgun man." He was believed responsible for at least one-third of the 38 unsolved Italian and Sicilian killings that took place there between January 1, 1910, and March 26, 1911. It is estimated there were between 60 and 80 Black Hand gangs working in Chicago at that time. (*See* Little Hell.)

Deuce and a Quarter
(*Black*) Buick 225. A car; wheels.

Ding
Hustle; mooch; bite. Like in "Put the ding on" someone. To panhandle in the street.

Dingbat
A TV hijack of a Chicago oldie. (Note use on "All in the Family" shows.) Originally, a southwest side colloquialism of the '20s meaning goofy, touchy, or quick-triggered—the latter in its literal sense. Became even more popular due to the early comic strip character by that name. Most notably applied to John "Dingbat" Oberta, the area's leading mobster and beer-runner. Dingbat Oberta was a partner of "Polack Joe" Saltis and Frankie McErlane—a very quick-triggered trio in the Roaring Twenties. (*See* Chicago Typewriter.)

Dog-Ass
In this city—the lowest of the low.

Door Knocker
A private eye, a Pinkerton, especially a watchman with a regular route, who checks to make sure the doors are locked after business hours.

Dot Head
East Indian. Pakastani.

Double Bubble
Originally a hooker's term for handling two johns at the same time or in the process of the same trick. Now, two of anything for the price of one, or an accidental extra score: like in knocking over a bank and making the bank president for his pinky ring on the way out.

Double-Dippin'
Holding two political jobs at the same time—feeding twice from the public trough.

Downtown
Very heavy political clout or leverage. Also, the real inside dope, as in "Dis came right from *downtown*, know what I mean?" (*See* Fif' Floor.)

Dukey
Brown bag lunch.

Eighty-Six
Chicago bartenders' traditional term for the cutoff. The heave-ho. You've had enough to drink.

11th Ward

Bridgeport's ward. Longtime home and power base of the Irish politicians whose machine and patronage army control Chicago's city and (Cook) county government. Past Mayors Kelly, Kennelly, Daley, and Bilandic all came out of these clannish precincts. (Byrne didn't come from there; she came from Daley's knee.) Many political analysts feel that John Kennedy owed his presidential victory margin to the machinations of this single ward. (*See* Bridgeport, Cemetery Vote, Clout, Stinger, etc.)

Equalizer

(Trad.) Gun. Especially a handgun. "Be not afraid of any man who walks the streets of the city. Though he be large, and you be small, I will equalize."

Faust

BS. A fairy tale. A fast line.

Fence Jumper

(Hood) A button man or made man who transfers his allegiance from one outfit or crime family to another.

Fif' Floor

(Polit.) The inner sanctum; the holy of holies. In City Hall the fifth floor is the office of the mayor and hence the epitome of clout. "Dis came direct from the fif' floor, Charley, *see?*"·

Gaff

(Hood) A scheme or a pitch. Sometimes, loosely, a scam. Any operation of a larcenous nature. A hustler's MO (Modus Operandi), or road game, can be called his gaff. Frequently used as in, "What's the gaff?" meaning "What's in it for me?" (*See* Scam, Sting, Murphy Man.)

Gaffer

The bagman or the guy who comes around to make the protection or juice collection, often for the police captain in the district, for splitting up later. Also, loosely, a political insider or local heavyweight; the man to see. (*See* Bagman, Captain's Man, Juice.)

Gary, Indiana

(Cops) Refers to a character with a sketchy, shady, or foggy history. A guy you can't get a "make" on (see definition). Often describes a newcomer, small-timer or nonentity; "Who's the new dude, Maxie?" "I dunno, kid, he's from Gary."

Gimmick

(Trad.) Although Webster's still lists it as "orig. unknown," this is another Chicago oldie that is now in general usage. The word was first used by Chicago coin machine mechanics, back in the '30s, to describe the tiny

weights they attached to the inner wheels of slot machines. These weights controlled the odds for payout. With more than 8,000 different combinations possible, gimmicks could make the machines payoff 70–30, 60–40, 50–50, 40–60, 30–70—whatever the operator wanted for a particular location. Usually, the payout was fat when the machine was first installed, to encourage play. (*"What's the gimmick?"*) Chicago, then as now, is the gambling hardware capital of the world. Mills Novelty was founded here in 1897; Bally, today's mega-giant, in 1931. Most are still influenced by the outfit in some way, if not controlled outright.

Go East 'Til Your Hat Floats
Get lost. (The lake is to the east.)

Go into Your "A" Game
Give it your best shot. Give it some effort.

Gold Coast

Chicago's lakefront window dressing. High-rise, high-rent condo living à la Father Dearborn. Start looking at Michigan Avenue and Oak Street, 1000 north. Follow Michigan as it joins with Lake Shore Drive and winds out to approximately North Avenue, at 1600. That's Chicago's classic old Gold Coast. Most of the great mansions that gave it its name, like the McCormick castle, are long gone; but you'll still *see* some posh residences and high-rises. Don't peek too far behind it, though. Immediately to the west you'll run into some pretty grim slums. (*See* Streeterville, Magnificent Mile.)

Goo-Goos

City Hall name for the good government crowd, the city's reformer groups. Usually, these are wealthy liberals from the suburbs, lakefront, and Gold Coast—and Chicago has always had them to spoil the fun.

The BGA (Better Government Association) and the League of Women Voters, for example, are goo-goos. They wield little direct political power here—they don't have the vote. For some reason, however, they always seem to terrify the downtown cigar chompers, who do have the vote. "Play it cool today, Dominick, I jest got word from downtown another goo-goo delegation is comin' over." Unless there is a very heavy political scandal, the best the goo-goos can do is influence an occasional election in one of the lakefront wards.

Gray Wolves
(Trad.) The City Council. Chicago's aldermen.

Greaseball
Any Latino, Italian, or Greek. Anybody who doesn't look like a WASP.

Greaser
Hamburger, especially from a fast-food joint.

Greasing
(Black) Eating.

Greek Lightning
(Cops/Hoods/Fire Dept.) Arson. A fire set for insurance purposes. Especially a fire in a restaurant that is losing money—like in a Greek joint where the gyros ain't selling.

Greek Town
The city's original old Greek Town is now mostly a restaurant colony. The rich-smelling old family stores, with their barrels of ripe olives and their pita breads ... the gentle, bearded old men playing pangini ... are now mostly a memory. But you can still find some good *"O-pah!"* and a fine meal for your money. And belly dancing. Go to Halsted and Jackson, just southwest of the Loop, and look in any direction. Try Roditys, on the west side of Halsted—warm, lovely, you can't go wrong. There's a newer Greek Town north, also good, around Lincoln-Lawrence and Western avenues, 4800 north. (*See* Six Corners.)

Guinea
(Polit.) An Italian. Mostly applied to the earlier generation of immigrant laborers who swept the city's streets, a disproportionate number being of Italian extraction. (That's because "Diamond Joe" Esposito, a Little Italy political power, controlled the union.)

Hawk
(Black) The city's relentless cutting wind in the winter.

Heater and Cooler
Shot and a beer. In some sections, called a Polish martini. In others, called Irish pop.

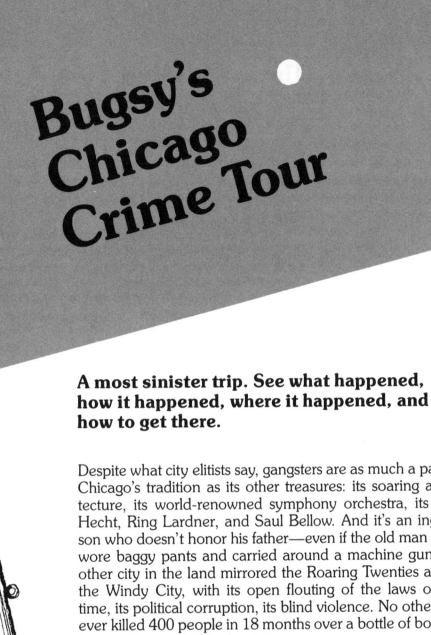

Bugsy's Chicago Crime Tour

A most sinister trip. See what happened, how it happened, where it happened, and how to get there.

Despite what city elitists say, gangsters are as much a part of Chicago's tradition as its other treasures: its soaring architecture, its world-renowned symphony orchestra, its Ben Hecht, Ring Lardner, and Saul Bellow. And it's an ingrate son who doesn't honor his father—even if the old man once wore baggy pants and carried around a machine gun. No other city in the land mirrored the Roaring Twenties as did the Windy City, with its open flouting of the laws of the time, its political corruption, its blind violence. No other city ever killed 400 people in 18 months over a bottle of bootleg booze. Or cared less about it.

Here are six happenings from that era, plus two more that helped it along. Included are on-the-spot photos of the events, which will take you back to the old days. Match 'em with photos of your own of how these spots look today. Take home a piece of the real Chicago—one you won't find in the guidebooks!

29

The St. Valentine's Day Massacre

"Bugs" Moran bugged Al Capone. He bugged him just as Dion O'Banion and Hymie Weiss, the previous leaders of the north side mob, had bugged Capone before they were eliminated. The Morans were the last holdouts, preventing the Big Fellow's complete control of the city. On a cold St. Valentine's Day in 1929, Al sent Bugs a love note.

A light snow was falling as the black Cadillac "police" car—complete even down to the police insignia painted on the side and the gong on the running board—pulled up at the S-M-C Cartage Company on north Clark Street. Two "policemen" got out and went in, followed by three other men in plain clothes. Seven Morans were inside, waiting for what they thought was a shipment of hijacked booze from Detroit at a bargain price. Thinking this was just another pinch, they obediently lined up against the garage wall, hands up.

Later, people outside the garage said it sounded like a pneumatic drill. The machine guns sprayed death three times—first high, then medium, then low. The bodies fell, twisting and jerking spasmodically. The two "policemen" then led the three "plainclothesmen"—the hit men—out of the garage and back to the Cadillac. The plainclothesmen had their hands in the air, in a traditional Chicago prohibition-raid style.

They missed Bugs. He was running late that morning. But after Big Al's love note, he was through in the city. Big Al? He had the perfect alibi: he was in Florida. Now he had all the cookies.

From the Loop, go straight north on Clark Street, to 2122, on the west side of the street, just past Armitage. The garage has long since been torn down, though you can still see two remaining white pillars if you look closely. The site is now occupied by a senior housing center, set back from the street. Al would have liked that. He liked to retire people, too. Permanently.

Chicago Tribune photo

Chicago Historical Society photo ICHi–14406

The Shooting of John Dillinger

He was the real-life Bogart of crime, long before Bogey portrayed him on the screen. Like Pretty Boy Floyd and Bonnie and Clyde, Dillinger was a folk hero to millions during the Depression—the millions who didn't like banks any more than he did. He had a weakness for women, though. And it was a woman who betrayed him, Anna Sage, the "woman in red." She was blood-red for John Dillinger.

After tipping off the feds, Sage accompanied John to the Biograph Theatre, on Lincoln Avenue, along with another girl, Polly Hamilton. *Manhattan Melodrama,* a gangster flick starring Clark Gable, one of John's favorites, was playing. Walking out after the movie, he spotted the Feds. But it was too late. Pulling his gun, he ran for it, heading for an alley a few yards south of the theater. Melvin Purvis and his G-men riddled him with bullets, and he fell, half in and half out of the alley.

It's all still there. The Biograph Theatre and the alley, though the bloodstains are gone. They were sopped up on the spot by souvenir lovers with hankies. Take Lincoln Avenue north to the Biograph, 2433 N. Lincoln Avenue, just past Fullerton. Don't forget your camera.

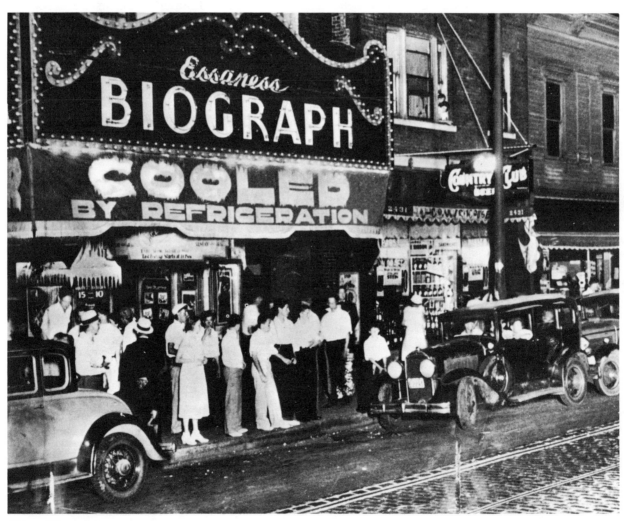

Chicago Tribune photo

Dion O'Banion and the Flower Shop Hit

"Tell them greasy Sicilians to go to hell," said the strutting little Irishman with the limp. It wasn't a smart thing to say about your business competition in the Chicago of prohibition days. While a little hijacking, price cutting, or maybe even a potshot or two was part of the game, an outright ethnic slur was not. This could be satisfied only by blood. But O'Banion, the north side chieftain, was a weird gangster even by Chicago standards. For one, he was a flower fancier. He bought himself a floral shop. He was gangland's official florist, no small business in itself in those days.

He was expecting the three swarthy Gennas who walked into his shop the morning of November 10, 1924. Mike Merlo, president of the *Unione Siciliane*, had died and they were to pick up the floral piece they had ordered for his funeral. Mike Genna, ("Il Diavalo"—Mike the Devil), solemnly extended his hand. O'Banion took it. Yes, their order was ready. Suddenly, Mike the Devil jerked the Irishman forward, off balance. The other two men, John Scalisi and Albert Anselmi, pumped five slugs into his body. Plus one more, the *coup de grace*, into his mouth. This *braggadocio* would talk no more. Let him bleed into his flowers.

The spot is only minutes from the Loop. Take State Street north to Chicago Avenue, 800. O'Banion's florist shop was at 738 N. State, on the west side of the street, about halfway between Chicago and Superior, the first street south. There's a parking lot there now. Wouldn't you know?

Double Bubble. It's a rich block for crime buffs! Hymie Weiss, who took over the O'Banion mob, was gunned down across the street from O'Banion's old shop, in front of the Holy Name Cathedral, which is still standing. Capone had machine gun nests in second floor flats on Superior, covering both sides of State. If you look closely, you still can see the bullet pockmarks on the cathedral.

Chicago Tribune photo

Terrible Tommy's Bust-Out

His gallows waited for 50 years, carefully stored in the basement of the old Criminal Courts Building at Hubbard and Dearborn. But they were never used. Four days before he was to swing, December 21, 1921, Terrible Tommy O'Connor went over the wall and disappeared into the back alleys of nearby Little Hell (see definition in Chicago-ese dictionary).

O'Connor, a terrorist, burglar, and killer from the old Bloody Maxwell Street District, was to die for the gunning down of detective Paddy O'Neil. After his escape he was the object of Chicago's biggest manhunt ever. The old Criminal Courts Building, made of quarried rock, and a fascinating reminder of Chicago's past, is still standing and still in use as an administration building. Take Dearborn north, out of the Loop, to Hubbard, a few short blocks. You can't miss it. Abutting it, to the north, is a modern firehouse. It stands on the old prison exercise yard, which Tommy ran across, after dropping out of a window on that side of the building.

Double Bubble. This nostalgic old building also held Loeb and Leopold, in their 1924 "Crime of the Century." Ben Hecht and Charles MacArthur, as reporters, used it as background for their play, *The Front Page*.

Chicago Tribune photo

Capone's Fortress—The Hotel Metropole

This grim seven-story bastion was the operational headquarters for the biggest organized criminal assault on society in the nation's history. Located at 2300 S. Michigan Avenue, conveniently close to both Central Police Headquarters and City Hall. Big Al maintained more than 50 rooms here, some for living and everyday business, others set aside for gambling and prostitution.

Sunday mornings were especially busy times at the Metropole. Sunday was payday for graft and the place teemed with uniformed police, politicians, gamblers, pimps and hangers-on of every description. Women roamed the halls, as easily accessible as the sumptious food and liquor stocked in the hotel. Payoffs were in cash, the whole business being conducted as openly as a State Street department store.

The building was torn down a few years ago, and today it's just a large vacant lot. The wreckers looked but never did find the secret escape tunnel Scarface had installed, which was also used to get rid of embarrassing bodies. You might try your luck. The tunnel was rumored to surface in the alley, just northwest of the hotel, in the 2200 block.

Take Michigan Avenue straight south out of the Loop to 2300. The Metropole was on the southwest corner. And when you leave *that* piece of sanctified ground, you're just a few steps from the roots of organized crime in Chicago itself.

Chicago Tribune photo

34

Big Jim Colosimo's/The Four Deuces

It was the biggest and gaudiest nightclub of the day. Few headliners playing Chicago failed to put in an appearance at Colosimo's: George M. Cohan, Al Jolson, Galli-Curci, Caruso. But word was out that Big Jim Colosimo was going soft. For one, he had dumped his fat Italian procuress wife, Victoria, who had set him up in the whorehouse business and made him wealthy, and married a young singer he had fallen for. "It's your funeral, Uncle Jim," said his nephew, Johnny Torrio. Colosimo had brought in the wily Torrio from New York to manage the business—his bagnios, labor rackets and nightclub.

In fact, Big Jim was so blinded by his new love that he couldn't see the millions to be made by the passage of the Volstead Act. But Torrio could. Torrio, himself, had even imported a young tough from Brooklyn, one Alphonse Capone, alias "Al Brown," to give him a hand.

They found Colosimo with a bullet hole in his right temple, in the vestibule of his cabaret, May 11, 1920, and the gangster era had arrived.

From the Metropole site on Michigan Avenue, walk a short block west to Wabash. Go north on Wabash to 2126, where Colosimo's once stood. The site is now occupied by, wouldn't you know, another parking lot. There's a B-B-Q joint on the corner.

Double Bubble: Walk back (south) on Wabash, about a block and a half, and you'll be in front of the old Four Deuces, so named because it was at 2222 S. Wabash. The site is now occupied by—you guessed it—another parking lot. This notorious brothel and gambling dive was where Al Capone broke in as a pimp and strong-armer for Johnny Torrio. Later he managed the place. At least 12 gangsters were known to have been killed in the Four Deuces. Many were worked over under the EL structure behind it.

Chicago Tribune photo

The Everleigh Club/The Levee

The gold leaf piano was valued at $15,000. The gold spittoons alone cost $650 each—and that was in 1900. The most ornate sin palaces of Paris, New York, and San Francisco were hovels compared to this elegant, three-story, 50-room *bagnio* to end all *bagnios* at 2131–2133 S. Dearborn Street. Chicago's gay blades threw money like rice at a wedding at the Everleigh Club. And the two aristocratic sisters who ran it, Ada (left) and Mina (right), retired wealthy.

From the Four Deuces, go back north a few steps to 22nd Street. Turn left (west) on 22nd and walk a short distance to where Dearborn Street *would* come through. It no longer does. But it's easy to track. You'll see a sidewalk on the right (north) side of 22nd that leads into a covered walk. The walk, in turn, leads into an entranceway of one of the buildings in the Raymond M. Hilliard Housing Project. That's the site of the old Everleigh Club. Get your camera out.

Double Bubble: The site of the old Everleigh Club also puts you in the heart of what was once the wicked, wicked Levee (see definition). Stop and take a nostalgic look at the age of the dark and the corrupt. Wind up your tour with a bite at one of the great eateries in adjoining Chinatown (see definition).

Chicago Tribune photo

Chicago Historical Society photo

Little Italy

Don't miss old Little Italy, where much of it started. Walk rich Chicago ground! Home of the Black Hand and the bloody 19th ward, the flowering of the American Mafia (although *our* Italian gangsters never called it that. *Mafia* was a later newspaper term). Center of the Genna alky-cooking industry, long before Capone came in, caught the scent, and became czar. Cradle of the notorious "forty-two" gang, neighborhood punks of the '30s, many of whom later graduated to syndicate leadership, notably Sam Giancana.

The old center of Little Italy was at Taylor and Halsted streets, just southwest of the Loop. (For purists, much of the early Italian colony was located just east of there, an area now occupied by factories, the University of Illinois, and the Dan Ryan Expressway.) But for your tour, start at that corner, maybe dropping in to visit the Jane Addams Hull House reconstruction, which is just north on Halsted. It's a fascinating mini-museum of the settlement. From there, go west on Taylor to 1022. That's the site of the old Genna warehouse, now a vacant lot next to a fast-food eatery. Here is where the six "Terrible Genna" brothers collected their raw alcohol from hundreds of neighborhood cookers, cut it, dyed it, bottled it, and shipped it out, often under paid police escort.

From there, continue west on Taylor to Racine. Take in some of the side streets. There's still some of the old ethnic flavor left—period frame houses and some breathtaking old-world churches. (Visit the Holy Family, at Roosevelt and May.) Stop at the Italian bakery on Taylor just before you get to Racine, for some homemade cannolini. Have an Italian ice. Eat some *real* Italian food, at honest prices, almost anywhere in the area (see definition of Little Italy).

Chicago Tribune photo

Heavy
Exceptionally powerful clout, very close to the fif' floor (see definition). Your brother-in-law is a ward committeeman. Your uncle is Charley Swibel's banker.

Herb
(Black) Marijuana. Pot, ganj, grass, weed, etc.

Hero
A city fireman.

Hinky-Dink
(Trad.) Flimsy, jerry-built. Of a suspicious nature. Probably a corruption of the name of an early cartoon strip character, "Rinky Dink." Here, forever the nickname of Michael "Hinky-Dink" Kenna, co-alderman and master boodler of the old 1st ward, along with his partner, "Bathhouse John" Coughlan. The 1900 "Lords of the Levee," Kenna and Coughlan had a piece of everything, including the infamous Everleigh Club. (See Levee, Gray Wolves, Everleigh Club.)

Hitting the Bricks
On the street, broke, out of a job.

Hubbard's Cave
Section of the Dan Ryan expressway, between Randolph and Ohio streets, as it runs under the Chicago and Northwestern tracks. Noxious and nerve-wracking. Don't get caught dead down there.

Hustle
To con, essentially for a living. A "light" con is usually something fairly harmless, as compared to a jailable offense. (See Sting, Scam, Mark.)

Injun Country
(Cops) 63rd and 65th streets, south of the Loop, west of the lake. Tough turf. Don't get caught dead down there, either.

Italian Mausoleum
Car trunk.

Jacket
(Hood/Polit.) A frame. The squeeze. "To put the jacket on" somebody is to make him the fall guy. Usually put on a political job holder or criminal. And in Chicago there isn't always that much difference. (See Trick Bag, Vise.)

Jingle Bell Crew
(Cops) Pickpocket team. Now mostly applied to the professionals from Colombia, South America, the city's most adroit. The term comes from the way they practice their craft: attaching bells to clothes dummies, which jingle when they "clumsy up" the lift.

Johnson Family
(Hood) To be a member of the Johnson Family is to believe everything is on the up and up. You are a square john. You even trust your ward committeeman. You are ripe for the plucking.

Jug
(Cops/Hood) A bank.

Juice
(Hood) Another Chicago-ese contribution to the mother tongue. Originally usury on a gangland loan, it has now been broadened to include practically any skim, scam, or payola—money off the top. In New York it's called *vigorish*, or just *vig*. (*See* Skim, Scam, Bagman.)

Kelly's Follies
(Trad.) The weird, fender-bending 180-degree turns on the Outer Drive, just south of the Chicago River. This man-made obstacle course is a legacy from Mayor Ed Kelly, a Bridgeport boy, who conceded some rather strange rights to the railway people, who owned the land underneath. (These curves now being straightened out with taxpayer money.)

Kid
(Hood) A punk. A soldier or button man not yet made. A gofer.

Kiss-Off
(Hood) Successful completion of a sting or scam. The "walk-away" with the mark's money. (*See* Sting, Scam.)

Knock
A drink.

Kup
Irv Kupcinet, *Chicago Sun-Times* gossip columnist. Follow the celebrities in "Kup's Column." Find out what's happening in town and to whom.

Levee
Chicago's old redlight district, "toughest west of the Barbary Coast." Home of the Everleigh sisters, House of all Nations, Bucket of Blood and Big Jim Colosimo. Fiefdom of Bathhouse John and Hinky-Dink. Springboard for Johnny Torrio and Al Capone's eventual citywide empire of crime. In its heyday an incredible conglomerate of door-to-door gambling halls, clip joints, barrelhouse saloons, and more than 500 whore-houses. Take Clark Street, as it runs south out of the Loop and becomes Wentworth. The area peaked at around 18th–22nd streets, taking in a maze of side streets and alleys. Mostly blight today, but you can still walk its vice-soaked ground. Have a good meal at any number of great places in adjoining Chinatown. (*See* Bugsy's Crime Tour and map.)

Lifted

(Polit.) Eased out of your job, usually replaced by a guy with heavier clout; i.e., a guy with a bigger Chinaman.

Light

(Polit.) A payroller who is easily lifted (see definition). One without too much clout or smarts. "'Joey is a nice kid but he's light as a cork.''

Lincoln/DePaul

Once a part of the old "near nort' side"—a heavy German-burgher-homeowner-shopkeeper neighborhood. At first glance, you might think this area is an extension of nearby Old Town, but it's a far cry. Much younger, more congenial, more down-to-earth crowd and doings. Interesting taverns, good beer. Fine music—folk, jazz, blue grass, you name it. Good little theater. Some university influence just to the west (DePaul University). Hardly anyone gets shot here. Most of the play is on Lincoln Avenue, from Armitage, 2000 north, through Fullerton, 2400, to around Diversey, 2800. (*See* map.)

Listed

(Polit.) Out of favor. On Mr. Big's shit list, or in the process of getting canned or demoted. Such as a cop getting consigned to a beat in the boonies.

Little Hell

AKA "Smoky Hollow." Chicago's original "Hell's Half Acre," an early Irish shantytown with a mind-blowing crime rate even by this city's standards. This half-mile-square, near north side cesspool, crammed with more than 30,000 poor, was fenced in by Grand and Chicago avenues on one side and Clark Street and the river on the other. The chief occupation of its inhabitants, who called themselves "Kilgubbins," consisted of muggings, mayhem, and murder, when they were not engaged in such lighter pursuits as cooking rotgut Irish poteen from potatoes, brawling, cop fighting, purse snatching, and prostitution. Dion O'Banion, Capone's perennial Irish problem, came out of Little Hell. After 1900, Sicilian and Italian immigrants began pushing in, adding to the fun and games, and eventually turning the area into a "Little Italy north." There's not much left of the old place anymore. The old Liberty Inn, on Clark Street, where young O'Banion worked as a singing waiter when not jack-rolling drunks, was reopened as a gay joint for a while and renamed O'Banion's. The original building is still up, at this writing. (*See* Bugsy's Crime Tour, the O'Banion Hit.)

Little Italy

Old Italian quarter, once centered around Taylor and Halsted streets, just southwest of the Loop. Once a crowded maze of tenements, small stores and factories, pushcarts and narrow, garbage-strewn streets. A

giant slum redolent with the smells of garlic, pasta, fresh bread, wine-mash and raw alky. Cradle of many of Chicago's famous and infamous, from civic leaders and federal judges to the toughest gangsters of the Roaring Twenties. This is where "Diamond Joe" Esposito, fixer for boot-leggers, gamblers, and vice-mongers, dispensed jobs to the neighbor-hood poor. Where the six "Terrible Genna" brothers ran their "cottage industry" for the making of illegal alky, hundreds of *paesani* were cook-ing it in basement, kitchen, and bedroom. Where Jane Addams, a lone beacon, founded and operated Hull House.

There's not much left of this rich slice of ethnic Chicago, either. It was largely razed and fractionated by the same University of Illinois complex, and expressway, that did in nearby Greek Town and Maxwell Street. You might want to visit Hull House. The (preserved/reconstructed) ad-ministration building is still there—although somewhat lugubriously moved to the former site of "Diamond Joe's" notorious *Bella Di Napoli* cafe. See Old Chicago. Explore some great, checkered-cloth eateries. Try Gennero's, at Taylor and Racine, or the Vernon Park Inn, on Vernon Park, where late mob boss Sam Giancana liked to eat his lunch. Shed a tear while there. (*See* maps and Bugsy's Crime Tour.)

Loop
For the totally uninitiated, this is the city's core downtown area. The white-collar working, shopping, administrative hub of the city and (Cook) county; trading and financial center of the Midwest. Called the *loop* because of the ancient (80-year-old) "EL" structure that completely girdles it. Super shopping. Walk the new State Street Mall. But see it during the day; stay away from it after dark. Despite the promotional efforts of Mayor Byrne and the merchants, it pretty much dies after seven o'clock anyway. Crime buffs: pause on Madison Street, in between State and Dearborn, for a moment of silence. Here Tony Lombardo, president of the *Unione Siciliane* and a Capone *consigliere*, got his in broad daylight. Probably the city's most public gangland execution—thousands looked on with typical big-city stoicism. (*See* Maps.)

Lost an Eye
(Hood) Didn't pay his juice on time.

Lost His Hat
(Hood) Got himself hit—trunked.

Lugan
Lithuanian.

Lujack
(Polit.) To pass the buck. To slide deftly out from under a charge, while simultaneously sandbagging somebody else. Not to be confused with one of Chicago's more prominent disc jockeys, Larry Lujack.

Lunch
Finis—there ain't no more. "He got his lunch."

Madame
Extortion victim.

Maggie Murphy
The giant gilded statue of Columbia, in Jackson Park, on the south side. A relic of the 1893 Chicago World's Fair.

Magnificent Mile
The city's front yard. Chamber of Commerce tag for the showplace of department stores, haute shops, hotels, high-rises and bistros on Michigan Avenue north. Runs from the river to Oak Street, 1000 north. Most of the communications industry is here, too; called "Ad Row." Bring plenty of money. (*See* Streeterville, Gold Coast.)

Make
(Cops). Identify. Get a *make* on a law-breaker. Also *(Hood),* to hit a good score. Knock over a joint.

Man
(Black). The cops.

Mark
(Hood). Hustler or con man's victim or intended victim. The guy to be set up for the Sting. (*See* Sting, Scam, Shooting the Grease.)

Johnny Torrio

"Machine Gun" Jack McGurn

Jake "Greasy Thumb" Guzik

Max Von Hinten

(Ger.) Literally, "Max from the rear." Old near north side German street expression meaning a sneaky guy or a thief—one who enters from the rear. Also, sometimes used to describe a gay, i.e., a sodomist.

Maxwell Street

What's left of Chicago's once-colorful Jewish slum and sidewalk bazaar, just southwest of the Loop. Still open for business. You can get seconds and mildly hot goods here, but now mostly a freak show. Take Halsted Street south to Roosevelt Road (12th Street) and walk a block south. Eat a real kosher hotdog before this area is also destroyed by urban renewal. *(See Little Italy, Greek Town.)*

McInery

(Polit.) Last gasp—the death rattle. What happens to old politicians in Chicago. Comes from an early west side Irish undertaker of that name. "Put up the lace curtains and call McInery, Maggie, I think I've come to the end of life's journey."

Mickey Finn

(Trad.) *Webster's* blows the origin of this hoary Chicagoism, too. They list it as "unknown." A little digging would have told them that this heady concoction was first brewed here by, you guessed it, Mickey Finn. Finn, born in Ireland, was a pimp, strong-armer, pickpocket, and all-around thief. He operated the Lone Star Inn, a dive on Harrison Street's "whiskey row" in the 1890s, near the old Levee. Mickey is said to have gotten the formula, basically a compound of hydrate of chloride plus various bar goodies, from a New Orleans "voodoo doctor" by the name of Hall. Finn slipped this to well-heeled customers. After they hit the deck, he dragged them into the back room and plucked them, with the help of his wife, Gold-Tooth Mary. *(See Levee.)*

Moll Buzzer

Pickpocket or pickpocket crew who prey on women.

Monkey Ward

(Trad.) Montgomery Ward, the department store/mail order house. A big city employer but never noted for its high wage scale.

Moustache Pete

First-generation Italian (or Sicilian) gangster. An old Mafioso, like the kind that play the "Godfather" roles in the late-night movies.

Murphy

(Cops) A con or hustle using sex as the come-on. They set up the mark with girlie procurement. Also, a hooker who promises a john sex, or extra sexual favors, collects and then leaves him holding his pants. She often works in cahoots with a pimp. *(See Murphy Man.)*

Murphy Man
(*Cops*) Con man who poses as a pimp. Collects and steers john to non-existent hooker, or uses girlie procurement to set up his sting. (*See* Murphy, Sting.)

Mr. Kibitsky
A west side alias. Mr. Kibitsky is a good joe. He's a member of the Johnson family (see definition).

New Town
Bohemian-north area, somewhat on the low-brow side. Lots of saloons, boutiques, ethnic eateries, antique shops, and avant-garde theater. The local theater talent is good. You can do a little snorting here, if you want to. Plenty to drink. Singles, swingles, sex—straight, bi, or gay. Wear your beat-up levis. Loosely begins around Clark and Fullerton, 2400 north, following Clark to Diversey, its hub where it branches off down Broadway and ends near Belmont. (*See* maps.)

Noodleman
(*South Side*) A lawyer. One who gets you out of a jam.

Old Town
Older, more traditional, more expensive version of New Town. Chicago's original hippie, with-it, flower-child scene; now getting a little long in the tooth and more laid back. Good expense-account steaks, folk music, street-carnival atmosphere. Enjoy *Second City*, incubator of original comedy artists Mike Nichols, Elaine May, John Belushi, etc. A lot of side street spillover along Clark Street and up on Armitage. Watch your billfold. Old Town follows Wells Street, from Division to around Armitage, center of the action at North Avenue. (*See* maps.)

On My Case
(*Black, originally*) Going out of your way to criticize, bug me. I'm number 1 on your hassle list.

On the Hoof
Walking.

On the Street
(*Hood*) Free or independent. Without connections, open to an interesting proposition. Also, a character on his uppers. Or a new parolee.

Only Suckers Beef
Chicago is a tough town and not interested in losers. Next to "where's mine?" that's the name of the game here. If you lose, take your lumps and don't bitch. Nobody is going to run a tag day for you.

Three More Quickie Tour Maps

The Loop.

For some reason, visitors to Chicago find it difficult to get a simple street map of the city's downtown area—unless they're willing to pay $15 or carry around an Atlas. This one will get you around. Just remember, the Loop is girdled by the EL tracks, and laid out flat, grid-fashion. (*See* definition of Loop.)

The Old Levee.

Chicago's old Barbary Coast, left over from another era! Not much to see here now. But be sure to tell everybody you've *been there*. (*See* definition of Levee.)

Lincoln/De Paul.

The real Chicago, as we keep saying, is in the neighborhoods. This is a fun neighborhood and hardly anybody gets shot there. Pick up Lincoln Avenue at Armitage, 2000 North, and follow it to Fullerton, 2400. That's the core. Stay on Lincoln to about 2800. Note the Biograph Theatre on the way. (*See* definition of Lincoln/DePaul.)

The Loop

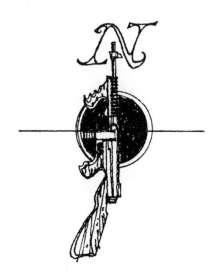

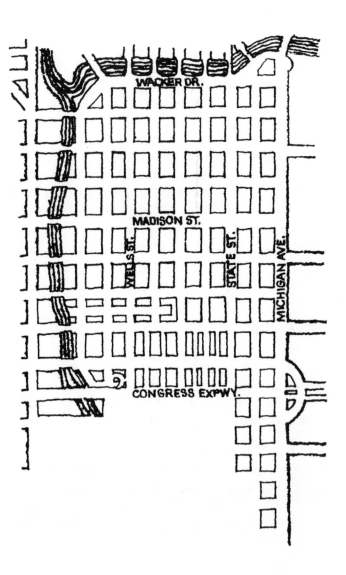

The Old Levee

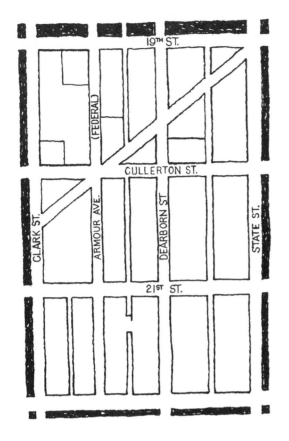

Lincoln/DePaul

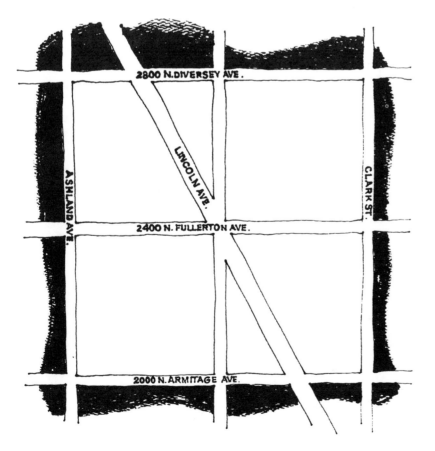

Outer Drive Hero

Any Chicago motorist who has survived five years of commuting on the expressways—the Dan Ryan, Eisenhower, Stevenson, Kennedy, Edens, Skyway, Calumet, or on the north-south Outer Drive.

Outfit

Syndicate, Mafia, Cosa Nostra, whatever. In this city it is usually and simply called the *outfit*. Despite hollers from city bigwigs—the late Mayor Daley swore it didn't exist—you'll be pleased to know that it's still doing business at the same old stand and operating just as efficiently as it ever did, if not as openly. In Chicago crime and politics forever share the same old bed. Only the names change, from year to year, to protect the guilty. The Capones, Torrios, and O'Banions of the '20s and '30s have been replaced by the Accardos, Giancanas, and Lombardos of the '60s, '70s, and '80s. It will be ever thus. The citizens made a pact with the devil when they started the thing here, back in Fort Dearborn days. The soldiers in the garrison screwed the Indians out of the whiskey they had promised them. The Indians retaliated by giving the settlers their lunch, out at 18th Street and the lake. But you wouldn't want it any other way, would you? What would you tell the folks back home? (*See* Hood's Who.)

Pass

Free ride. A literal cop-out, like in, "Jeez, officer, I was only doin' 50. I gotta wife and t'ree kids to support, and I work at Monkey Wards. Gimme a pass, willya?"

Penthouse

(Cops) The women's lockup on the top floor of the Central Police Headquarters, 11th and State streets. Here's where the cops store the hookers from the weekly Saturday night roundup. "The Midnight Follies." If the hookers are lucky, their pimps bail them out at court appearance next morning.

Petacque

Art Petacque, *Sun-Times* columnist. Chicago's successor to the famous reporter, Ray Brennan, on all things criminal and syndicate. Want to know who's stealing what here? He can tell you.

Pete

(Hood/Cops) A safe.

Peteman

(Hood/Cops) A safecracker or a burglar who specializes in opening or blowing safes.

Pilsen

At one time a "Lugan" immigrant neighborhood southwest of the Loop; now a booming Mexican *barrio*. A warm, colorful place featuring genuine Latino food and shopping. Mostly made up of good, hard-working people, some wetback, many poor, looking for their place in the melting pot. It can get a mite rough at night, especially for visiting *gringos* flashing too many *pesos*. Take the Dan Ryan, turn off at 18th Street, its main stem, and follow it west, past Blue Island.

Pineapple

(Trad.) A bomb, especially the old, and by today's standards almost nostalgic, hand-tossed bomb of the prohibition era. Originally called a *pineapple* because of its pineapple-like grenade configurations. Chicago has always been the nation's center for the manufacture of funny exploding devices, including illegal firecrackers. (*See* Bloody 19th.)

Pinky Ring

A fat rock, especially a diamond worn by aldermen, syndicate heavies, and other leading citizens.

Polish Matched Luggage

Two shopping bags from Goldblatt's. Goldblatt's, once the city's leading "cheap john" department store chain, recently declared bankruptcy and now operates a chain of discount stores.

Polk and Oak

Anyplace in the city you can't get to from anywhere. Polk and Oak both run the same way—same as Madison and Addison.

Punk

(Hood) A kid, especially any syndicate fringer not yet made. A guy who does not yet have his medallion. (*See* Button Man, Soldier.)

Queerborn Street

Dearborn Street, anywhere around Division.

Q.T.

(Hood) Mini-slot machine or other gambling device kept under the bar. Can be pulled out and placed on the bar for action—and quickly yanked back, should the heat or hijackers appear.

River Wards

(Polit.) The Democrat machine-controlled wards that follow the south-southwest branch of the Chicago River. These old vote plantations are held together largely by political patronage or, when the going gets tough, by outright vote purchase, guns, knives and baseball bats. On election night the tally of these wards is generally held back until the last moment, the plurality count carefully controlled to tip the scales in a close election. The River Wards tell you why you never see a Republican mayor in Chicago. Astute political observers will tell you that Chicago's River Wards probably put Kennedy in the White House in 1960—orders from Mayor Daley. (The River Wards delivered Chicago. Chicago carried Illinois. Illinois put Kennedy over.) (*See* Bloody 19th, 11th Ward.)

Royko

Want to *really* know Chicago and Chicago-ese? Read Mike Royko's syndicated column in the Sun-Times. He'll tell you where it is, where it's going, and to whom.

Rush Street

Glitter gulch. Expense account heaven. Nightlife sector that's big on name entertainment, T and A, and B-girl action. Some posh eateries. Pick up Rush just north of the Loop, one block west of Michigan Avenue. You might start at Chicago Avenue and follow the neons north to Division, 1200. Plenty of side-street play, especially on Wabash, Walton, Oak. Watch your credit cards. Don't get murphied (see definition). It's best not to drive or try to park. And, if you see a cat with a red bandanna handkerchief in his right hip pocket, know it's a gay "cruising" signal. The natives call Rush Street "the street of tears."

Rush Street Commando

A bust-out Italian with minor syndicate connections and lots of gold chains.

Salt Water

An Irish cop born in the "ould sod."

Scam

A legitimate operation taken over by an illegitimate one with the object of milking it. For example, Sam Swinger takes over Max Moola's 30-year-old jewelry business. Old Max is given a pretty good down payment for it, plus an investment in future growth. Using the old firm's name and credit line, Swinger orders $1 million worth of merchandise on the cuff. He sells the merchandise. He also turns everything else in the business into cash—anything that is cashable—and lams out. Max and the creditors are left holding the bag. Not to be confused with a sting or a skim. (*See* Sting, Skim.)

Dion O'Banion

Hymie Weiss

Bugs Moran

Sears Tower

World's tallest building. Big even for the city where they invented the skyscraper. On Wacker Drive, as it swings south. You can't miss it. Go up to the observation tower. See the whole beautiful, dark, and wonderfully corrupt place laid out before your eyes.

Shit Kicker

A rube, farmer, or hillbilly. (*See* Uptown.)

Shooting the Grease

(*Cops/Hood*) A con man's preliminary pitch, setting up his mark. (*See* Sting, Mark, Hustle.)

Shooting Star

(*Black*) A dude who comes on strong but fades fast.

Short Con

Bullshit. Light grease. Especially the kind used for setting up bar wagers, as compared to the professional act. Called "camel shit" on Rush and Randolph streets.

Short Dog

Half-pint of whiskey. (*See* Skid Row.)

Six Corners

While Chicago has many six-cornered intersections, one of the most interesting ones is at Lincoln, Lawrence, and Western avenues, on the north side, 4800 north. Unusual melding of new Greek Town and new Berlin. Chicago's great old ethnic neighborhoods are mostly a memory —fractionated, deteriorating, and antiquated. But you can still get a taste of them here. Drop into Meyer's Deli, just off the corners on Lincoln, for authentic Old World Kraut goodies. Eat in any of the Greek joints. This is no longer a true six-cornered intersection, due to the rerouting of Lincoln Avenue to make way for a mall.

Skid Row

Some say Chicago's whole inner city is a skid row, from its infrastructure on out; from its potholed streets, to its abominable transportation, to its inadequate housing for the needy. But that's a bum rap. And it doesn't apply to Chicago any more than it does to any of the other older, troubled cities in the northern frost belt. Actually, the city has two "classic" skid rows. Old, traditional skid row starts at Madison Avenue, just west of the Chicago River, and runs west for about a half-mile. New skid row starts at Clark and the river, and runs north to about Chicago Avenue, 800. Stay away from both.

Skim

(*Hood*) A percentage of the take siphoned off the top, as pure profit, before declaring earnings for tax purposes. Now used by many legitimate businesses, this Chicago syndicate-conceived ploy was originally devised for fattening their Las Vegas gambling take. The Chicago outfit has always had a strong, if covert hand, in Vegas gambling casinos.

Slurbs

The suburbs.

Sod Buster

(Cops) A business that looks legit on the outside but is phony on the inside. A "funny" operation. Also, an enterprise that isn't listed anywhere, doesn't have references, can't be checked out. Often a syndicate-operated front for concealing or laundering dirty money. Sometimes applied to a character without checkable references or a past. (*See* Scam; Gary, Indiana.)

Soldier

(Hood) A made man. Sometimes a hit man. An established member of the outfit who has earned his "medallion." (*See* Button Man.)

South-on-Stony

(Cops) Leaving town fast. Stony Island, a south side main street, takes

52

you directly out of the city heading south. "Last time I saw that mothah he was headin' south on Stony and carrying a big bag."

Spaghetti Bowl
The complex of streets, ramps, overpasses, and underpasses that meet and merge into the expressways just south of the Loop—the entrance and exits of the Dan Ryan, Eisenhower, and Kennedy. Even Chicagoans get apoplexy here. Don't drive it, unless you have your Outer Drive Hero's Badge.

Squadrol
Chicago name for a police squad car. (*See* Blue and White.)

Squeeze
To put the heat or pressure on, financially or politically. To use everything short of outright muscle to make your point. Sometimes, to muscle in on another's territory. (*See* Jacket, Vise.)

The Battlefield

Division of the Spoils/How the Gangs Cut Up Chicago in the '20s

Prohibition in Chicago produced many fantastic stories. But none more bizarre than the way the bootleg gangs sliced up the city into their own private baronies. The boundaries shown on this map are approximate. The battle lines shifted almost from day to day, depending on local alliances of convenience, political deals, and mob-figure assassinations, to say nothing of a constant merry-go-round of price cutting, hijacking, and outright raids into enemy territory.

Terry Druggan, for example, personally held Little Bohemia, a lucrative gin mill in the heart of O'Banion country. The Torrio-Capone Syndicate controlled Cicero and most of the west/southwest/south suburbs. They also maintained an uneasy alliance with the treacherous Gennas in Little Italy, for safe passage of their trucks and for the Gennas' raw-alky cooking facilities.

The Torrio-Capones, in addition, had detente arrangements with various local gangs who held small islands in the jungle: the Aiellos on the north side; the Claude "Screwy" Maddox circus gang and the Marty Guilfoyle mob on the northwest side; and, besides Ragen's Colts, Ralph Sheldon's cutthroats on the far south side. But here's about how it looked in the mid-'20s. By the end of the '20s, after the smoke cleared, Big Al had it all.

Far Northwest Side: Roger Touhy Gang.

North/Near North: Dion O'Banion/Hymie Weiss.

Loop/Central/South Side: Torrio/Capone Syndicate.

Little Italy/Near Southwest: Genna Brothers.

Near Southwest/West: Druggan/Lake Gang.

Southwest Side: Saltis/Oberta/Frankie McErlane.

South Side: The "Spike" O'Donnells.

South Side Island: Ragen's Colts.

West Side: The "Klondike" O'Donnells. (No relation to the "Spike" O'Donnells)

*Torrio-Capone Outlying Territories.

4200

2400

1600

ROGER TOUHY

NO MAN'S

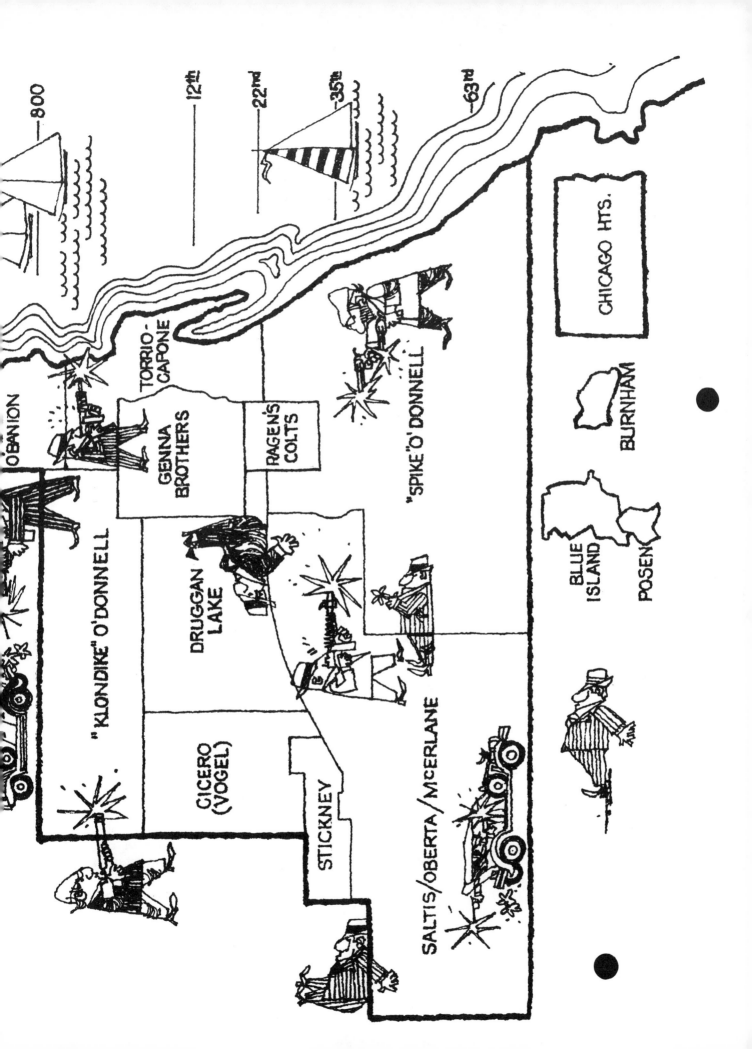

Stanley

A Pole.

Stiff

To cheat or connive, especially to stick somebody else with your responsibility or your share of the tab. Like, when the waiter presents the bill and asks you where your friend went: "That bum? He's no friend of mine. He orders three martinis, a big steak, and then stiffs me for the bill."

Sting

(*Trad.*) A very old term and original Chicago-ese. Now generic. Became popularized by the Oscar-winning movie of the same name. Now any con game is called a sting. Classically, the sting was not the entire caper; it was merely the first phase of the con operation, the laying in of the hook. Telling the mark he was going to get something for nothing. The movie, incidentally, was based loosely on a classic number pulled off by Joseph "Yellow Kid" Weil, dean of Chicago's confidence men, and his partner, Fred "The Deacon" Buckminister, around 1915.

Stinger

(*Polit.*) Illegal vote. Hoary Chicago political practice of voting a man twice, voting a vacant lot, counting an unregistered voter—any way to swing the precinct. (See Cemetery Vote.)

Straphangers

The city's public transportation riders—or victims. So called because of the ingenious system of straps that were once provided, to keep them upright and from being mashed, when no seats could be found during rush hours. Early Chicago transit robber barons, such as Charles Yerkes, always claimed their profits came from the straphangers; otherwise they just broke even. The situation hasn't changed much. Chicago still has one of the most pathetic public transportation systems in the nation. It's always broke, always a political football. If you really want to start a conversation with a stranger here, ask him or her about the CTA. Better to get ripped off by the cab drivers. (*See* "Taking a Chance.")

Streeterville

Historic near north lakefront area, specifically the piece of land enclosed by Grand Avenue on the south, Oak Street on the north, Michigan Avenue on the west, and the lake on the east. Named after "Captain" Streeter, the city's most famous squatter. Who *really* has claim to this multibillion-dollar piece of real estate? That's a good question. Years ago, after the Civil War, a big storm blew up on the lake. It washed Captain Streeter's beat-up old scow up on to shore, just north of the present Grand Avenue. With the boat a total wreck, Captain and his wife—forever called Ma—decided just to leave it there and set up housekeeping. The place looked as good as any. Eventually, over the years, the natural action of the lake built up fill around Cap's old scow and, together with other debris-and sand bars, began turning the area into a pretty sizable hunk of land. (Before Cap's man-made bottleneck, the lake washed up to today's Michigan Avenue.)

It was a wild, swampy stretch, but Cap claimed it as his own. Under his leadership it became a squatter's paradise—a lawless, rent-free jungle of shanties, whorehouses, and moonshine whiskey lean-tos. As the city grew and prospered and began spreading along the lakefront, land speculators began casting a greedy eye on Cap's acreage. Getting together, they bribed judges and law enforcement officials to tear down "Streeterville." It was an eyesore. But Cap, a feisty Civil War veteran and practically illiterate, fought back. He took the speculators to court. He declared his land the "Deestrict of Lake Michigan," a brand-new country that had never existed before, and promptly seceded it, not only from the State of Illinois, but from the Union as well. The real estate moguls, unable to win in court, put together a goon army and, reinforced by bought cops, attacked Streeterville. In the pitched battle that followed, Cap, with Ma at his side, fought 'em off with his ragtag army.

Cap won the first engagement but couldn't win the war. After numerous bloody battles and much real estate skullduggery, old Cap finally went down, shotgun blazing, and the squatters were evicted. Actually, legal ownership of what is now called Streeterville was fought out in the courts all the way until the 1930s. Cap and Ma were long since gone, but their heirs kept up the battle. Three guesses who won. Cap'n Streeter owning the Hancock building and the Drake Hotel? Now, that wouldn't be the *real* Chicago, would it? (*See* Magnificent Mile, Gold Coast.)

Studs
You'll hear the name while here. That's Studs Terkel, radio personality, author, and the city's liberal conscience. In many ways, Chicago-ese personified.

Styling and Profiling
(*Black*) Standing around and looking good; dressed sharp. Showing it off, particularly at a big ball or bash.

Taking a Chance
Taking public transportation. Chicagoans say you don't buy a ticket— you buy a chance.

TCB
(*Black*) Taking Care of Business. On the up and up. Playing it straight and cool. All the nines.

The Building
(*Hood/Cops*) Central Police District Headquarters, at 11th and State. The lockup.

The Club

There's only one "club" in Chicago. That's the prestigious Chicago Club on Michigan Avenue. Old wealth. A membership in the Chicago Club is a passport to financial success.

The EL

The antiquated overhead street railway system that provides the citizens with public transportation—sometimes. Chicago is one of the few remaining cities with overhead transportation. (*See* Taking a Chance.)

The Grove

Cottage Grove, a south side main stem. Black and beautiful. Hear some of the finest jazz in the city. Good theater, especially around the University of Chicago complex. Several fine soul food eateries. Well-mixed area. Don't go playing Honky games out there—you'll be the one who'll feel small.

The IC

Illinois Central Railroad. Provides south side and far south transportation into the Loop. Terminal at Michigan Avenue and East South Water Street in the IC building. Main commuter entrance is on Randolph.

The Islands

Goose, Stony, and Blue. Chicagoans call them *islands*, but, with the possible exception of Goose, they're really not islands. They're neighborhood and industrial areas. We wouldn't advise a tour of these scenic wonderlands, even if they are, in many ways, what "factory town" is all about. Goose can make it as an island, technically, because the area is enclosed by the north branch of the Chicago River and an industrial channel. (Originally called Goose because it was settled by immigrant Irish who raised flocks of geese there.)

The "Mare"

Chicago-ese for mayor, of course. Present fif' floor (see definition) occupant is Lady Jane Byrne, who sneaked in when her opponent couldn't get the snow off the streets. Called "Little Miss Bossie" by some, she's a tough, brainy gal. Can be vindictive and often inexplicably changes her mind, but she has won the grudging admiration of the professional pols. She learned her trade at the elbow of the master himself, Old King Richard.

The Three Ns

The city's three no-nos: "Never give matches to a Greek, whiskey to an Irishman, or power to a Polack."

The Parks

The town has any number: Albany, Douglas, Hyde, Jefferson, Kelvyn, Lincoln, Logan, Morgan, Rogers, Welles, Winnemac, and so on. Some have grass, trees, dog doo-doo and muggers. Others merely designate city areas. Stay with Grant Park, on the downtown lakefront, for great free concerts in the summer. And try Lincoln Park for a fine free zoo. Tread gingerly in the others, especially after dark.

The Patch

Once Irish and later Italian/Sicilian immigrant slum area merging into Little Italy on the west. A gang-ridden jungle at the turn of the century and tough turf right up into the '30s, '40s and '50s. Sam "Mooney" Giancana was one of its more illustrious graduates.

The Sag

Old Chicago Calumet Sag Canal. An industrial waterway southwest of the city. The name is short for "Ausoganananashkee," an early Indian name for a swamp in the area. Once a favorite dumping ground for one-way ride victims in the '20s.

Big Al's Boys Today

Chicago Crime Syndicate Update: Contrary to what the city fathers like to believe, organized crime is still one of Chicago's most dependable growth industries. Here's how the present outfit breaks down, as nearly as can be determined at this writing. Sudden and violent changes, in both upper eche-lon management and in personnel, are to be expected.

The Godfather

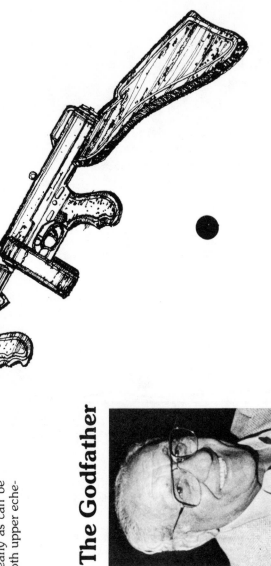

Tony "Big Tuna" Accardo. Alias "Joe Batters." Elder Statesman. Chairman of the Board emeritus.

General Sales Manager

Tony Spilotro

Capo Di Tutti Capi

Joey "The Doves" Aiuppa. Chief Operating Officer

Consiglieri

Jackie "The Lackey" Cerone

Capo Regimes

Vince Solano   Joey Lombardo   Joe Ferriola   Angelo La Pietra   Al Pilotto

Button Men

Joey DiVarco	Murray Jans	Phil Amato	Louis Aleman	Vince Inserra
Joe Arnold	Ray Caccamo	Chuck English (Ret.)	James Basile	Frank Butra
Jasper Campise	James D'Antonio	Frank Schweihs	Robert Salerno	Tom Scalise
Mike Glitta	Joe Pettit	Dom Motto	Mike Sarno	Leo Manfredi
Ken Etto	Larry Pettit	Dom Cortina	Sam London	Rich Catezone
Albie Frabotta	Chuck DiCaro	Don Angelini	Rich Piekarski	Sam Gallo
Frank DeMonte	Ron Covello	George Colucci	Joe Lamantia	Angelo Imparato
Orlando Catanese	Tom Covello	Bill McGuire	Ron Jarrett	Richard Lamantia
Tom Campione	James Cozzo	Joe Spadevechio	Frank Calabrese	Al Tocco
Frank Tornabene	Vic Spilotro	Ernest Infelice	Frank Caruso	Jim Pinckard
Sid Finzelbar	Nick Regilio	Wayne Bock	Morrie Caruso	Tony Pelligrino
Lenny Patrick	Pat Riciardi	Marco D'Amico	Tony Imparata	Chris Messino
Len Yaras	Joe Vento	Joe Greco	Terry Scalise	Roy Bridges
Ray Spencer	Frank Furio	Bernie Posner	Anthony Bova	Frank D'Andrea
Irv Kahn	Gerald Castino	John Varelli	Morton Geller	Jerry Ferraro
George Sommer	Mario Rainone	John DiFronzo	Sam Bills	Joe Scalise
Chris Serratella	Tom Fortiano	Arnold Garris	James LaPietra	Jerry Scarpelli
Dan Bartoli	James Mirro	John Manzella	John Monteleone	Tony Berretoni
Cal Sirkin	Mike Swiatek	John Copini	John Fecarotta	Joe Barrett
Arnie Taradash	Art Bravieri	Robert Cruz	Nick Montos	

Courtesy Chicago Police Intelligence Division/Chicago *SunTimes*.

The Sides

North, south, west. You'll find that most Chicagoans relate to their city, geographically, in terms of sides. So do the cabbies, cops, the public transportation system, and the phone books. You'll also discover that the city really has no east side. That's the lake. There actually *is* an east side, and east house numbers, as the city curves around the lake going south, but not to worry about it. Chicago is one of the easiest of all big cities to get around in. For example, there are no hills. The place is "flat as piss on a plate," as the natives say. The key to the whole caper lies at the intersection of State and Madison streets, in the Loop. All streets and buildings start being numbered at that corner; it's the baseline that divides the city into its three sides. All streets running north of Madison are designated north and so numbered—from 0 all the way to 7900 and the city limits. All streets running south of Madison are numbered south, in the same way, to the city limits. All streets running west of State, from the Madison corner, are numbered west. East numbers do pick up, east of State to the lake; but don't call this the east side—it's simply not in the city's lexicon and you'll confuse the citizens. *Tip*: If you're asking for directions, don't ask in Chicago-ese. Use your own alien tongue. The natives have a peculiar antipathy toward helping their own, but will knock themselves out for a stranger.

The Strip

Hotel, motel, nightclub, girlie-action along Mannheim Road. Just outside O'Hare airport, the world's busiest. Bring your credit cards. Get to know *the boys* while you're here.

The Valley

Once notorious lawless jungle centering around 15th Street, immediately south and west of the old Maxwell Street ghetto. An Irish immigrant slum at the turn of the century, featuring such characters as Paddy "The

Frank "The Enforcer" Nitti

Vincent "Schemer" Drucci

William "Klondike" O'Donnell

Bear" Ryan. Ryan, a waddling, five-foot, 250-pound obscenity, killed people by squeezing them to death. In the '20s, breeding ground of the Valley Gang, whose leaders, Terry Druggan and Frankie Lake, were celebrated beer barons of the prohibition era. Being sentenced to a year in jail for contempt of court did little to cramp the lavish lifestyle of this pair. When a reporter dropped around for an interview with Terry Druggan, the jailer told him: "Mr. Druggan is not in today." Abashed, the reporter then asked to talk to Frankie Lake. "Mr. Lake also had an appointment downtown," the jailer replied. "I will tell them you called. They will both be back after dinner."

The Yards
Old Union stockyards, now defunct. (See Back o' the Yards.)

Three More Ns
(City Hall) "Never give an answer when you can reply with a question." "Never say anything when you can wink your eye." "Never wink your eye when you can get away with bland silence."

Three Wheeler
Cop on a "bike." A Chicago traffic cop.

Trick Bag
(Black) To be conned. To be made a fool of or a patsy. On the south side you get "put into" a trick bag.

Tunnelman
(Cops) A burglar who specializes in going through walls or ceilings to make his score.

Turkey
An Irisher.

Twenty-Second and Wentworth
Solid political clout. Where you go to find political sponsorship—that's where Chinatown is. (*See* Clout, Chinaman, Chinatown.)

Union Depot
Old Chicago "IQ" question: where is it? If you don't know, you're generally tagged as a hayseed (though a lot of the new-breed Chicago cab drivers can't seem to find it). If some smart-ass *does* ask you where it is, tell him it's at Polk and Oak (see definition). Or Madison and Addison.

Uptown
Hillbilly north. A decaying area, much like the inner city, but sitting, untypically, far north. Bound, roughly, by Foster Avenue (5000), Montrose Avenue (4400), Ashland Avenue (2000 W), and the lake. A pathetic city locked within a city, plagued by high unemployment, arson, and police blotter-type crime. Also the city's Indian Reservation, mostly from northern Wisconsin tribes. A hard core of concerned residents work desperately to salvage it, but it's going fast. Don't go there. Why be depressed?

Vise

(Polit.) To put the screws to somebody. To "lever" somebody out of a job—to replace him with a friend. "Did you hear about Patsy? He got vised out by the alderman's brother-in-law."

West Side Passkeys

(Cops/Hood) Burglary tools. Pry bars. Essentially, burglary tools for breaking and entering.

Wheel Man

(Hood) Getaway driver. Key team man in any heist or hit. A good wheel man is seldom out of work in Chicago. Sam Giancana, the late Mafia Don, first caught the eye of the outfit as a hot wheel man with the old "42" gang. The "42s" were a collection of small-time west side punks who were good at stealing cars.

Willie

(Cops) A Black.

Woof

(Black) To bark at. To intimidate with your voice.